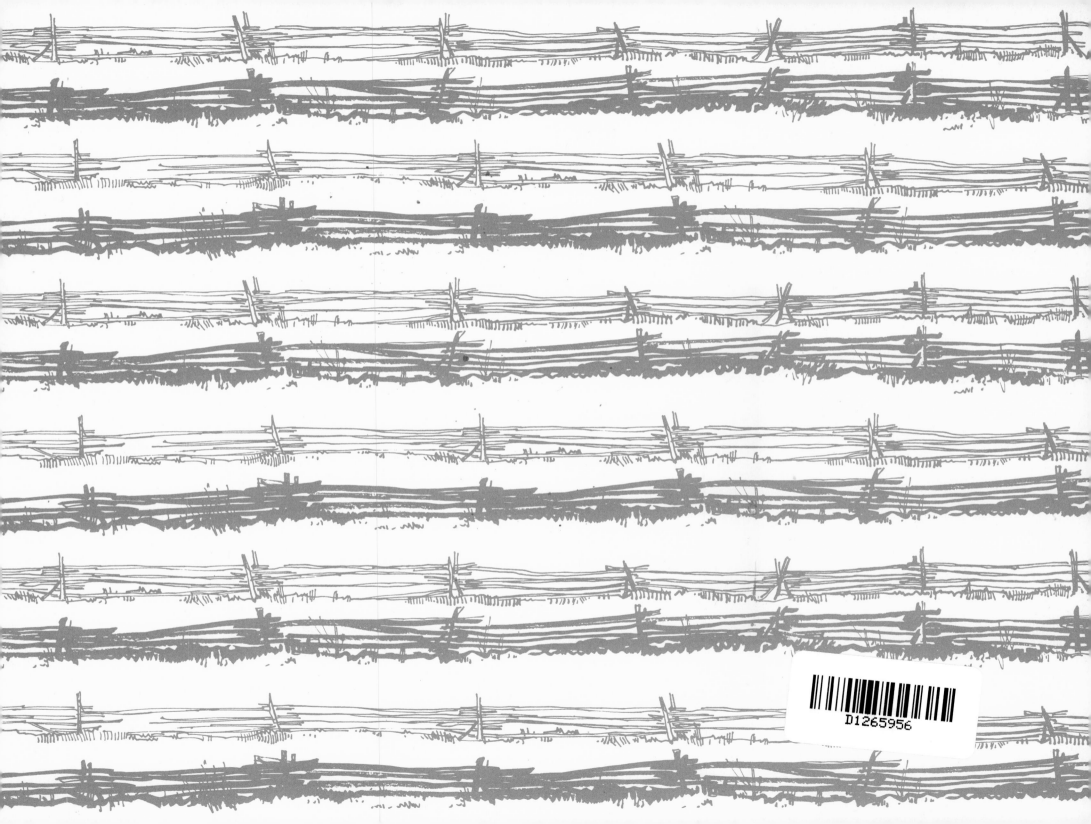

A Painter's Harvest

The Works of Peter Etril Snyder

A Peter Etril Snyder publication

Peter Etril Snyder
59 Erb Street East
Waterloo (Ontario), Canada
N2J 1L7

Canadian Cataloguing in Publication Data

Snyder, Peter Etril, 1944-
    A Painter's Harvest: the works of Peter Etril
Snyder

ISBN 0-88794-309-8

1. Snyder, Peter Etril, 1944-   . 2. Country life
in art. 3. Mennonites in art - Ontario.
4. Ontario in art. I. Title.

ND249.S6525A4 1986   759.11   C86-093888-3

Design: David Bartholomew

Printed and bound in Canada by Johanns Graphics Inc.

1 2 3 4 5 / 90 89 88 87 86

Introduction

Because I completed only three years of a four-year course at Ontario College of Art, it was impossible for me to follow the standard life-sustaining path that most academy-trained artists pursue. No school would hire me, no agency would hire me, no one would hire me. Because of that condition and not because of my inner fire, I was forced to develop an alternative to holding a job. Since fate had handed me an unusually rich topic — the Mennonites — I plunged ahead. It is important to consider that although a young artist may have a vision, it does not necessarily follow that he has the ability to develop that idea. My background gave me heavy input on the subject side, but that same background gave me no idea of cultural expression. Mennonites were not supposed to be artists and so my conditioning was totally against the very thing I needed.

As I look back over the last twenty years, I see the influences at work in my career. Because my father was in business, I absorbed the idea of building a small enterprise within the art area. Because magazines were one of the arresting influences in my childhood, it is not surprising that my work leans to the illustrative. Because our first trip to Europe twenty years ago followed so closely after the years at Ontario College of Art, I was able to connect classroom instruction about art history and theory with the originals that I saw in the galleries, in museums and in architecture. The traditional approaches to expression that I saw there struck a responsive chord from my conservative upbringing. Although I understood even at that point that painting for me was the description of a subject, any subject, it has taken a long time to develop those descriptive skills. Just as a writer makes notes and records bits of conversation, the artist learns to gather information together. Through drawings,

sketches, and photographs, I have built files containing over 25,000 pieces. Most of that information is photographic. Sometimes I do a drawing, paint a sketch and shoot a photograph of the same subject. These bits and pieces go into my file for further appraisal. People are quite surprised to see the items recorded there. A motorcycle, three rocks, a chicken, a truck's grill, some tiger lilies, a man rolling a cigarette — these are examples of the bits and pieces that I will someday call on as I build my tableaux. To develop a painting, I assemble a number of visual ideas which I organize to intensify or emphasize a particular effect. My paintings contain a major theme or idea around which I interweave four or five secondary items. In this book, I have isolated some of these secondary themes or ideas. I think the viewer may see particular motifs from my work in a new way. All my paintings are a combination of various pieces. Central for me is the setting, but once I have decided on that, other items are added to enhance either the logical idea or the aesthetic sense. Often when I am painting a commission I will be able to heighten the idea by the use of support information from my files.

Since my paintings are a pulling together of elements, I often find difficulty in adding and subtracting ideas. It has been said that it takes two people to do a painting, one to do the painting, the other to shoot him when it is done. Because I work with fast-drying acrylic paint, the option of rapid change is possible. I sometimes feel as I take a painting down from my studio wall where I have pinned it for a rest, that this is not a better painting than the version that I had two days ago, it is only different. At any time I have twenty paintings on the wall waiting for a hoped-for burst of inspiration.

i

Just as themes intertwine in a painting, the various subjects such as Mennonite life, country life, character studies, landscapes (local and foreign), still life, events, animal studies, and floral topics are constantly in my mind. I move freely in my work and may put touches on paintings of several different varieties the same day. I thought it reasonable, then, to organize this book in a flowing way. No titles or headings are used for groups of subjects. Although images on a spread (double page) are somewhat related either by subject of visual device, I hope to lead the viewer fluidly through this gallery of images which encompasses most of the topics that I currently paint.

This book is intended to introduce people to the variety of work that I have done over the past twenty years. Obviously this is only a group of examples, and a totally different book could have been composed, had I included other works. Because most people know my work only from reproductions and not from visits to my gallery in Waterloo, the public's perception is that my work is more heavily weighted to Mennonite paintings than it really is. Bit by bit as we publish more varied subjects, I hope that people will understand and enjoy the fact that for me any subject is just an excuse to paint.

Because I am a painter and not a writer I have kept the text to a minimum, but for those who wish further information a complete list of all the figures in this book has been placed at the back so as not to interfere with its visual pleasure.

Dedication

To my wife Marilyn who willingly sacrificed for my career and whose strong aesthetic sense inspired me.

To my brother Doug and the staff at our gallery in Waterloo whose attention to the day-to-day aspects of the art business makes it possible for me to be free to roam about and follow the muse.

To the public whose early and continuing support has allowed me to continue to develop.

I thank you all.

Although folk art is not encouraged among the Mennonites, some activities such as quilt making, embroidery, bird house-building, and general farm construction are fostered. To all acceptable activities there must be an element of utility. Occasionally a frivolous item such as a whirligig slips through the strong self-imposed net of practicality.

3

7

8

11

10

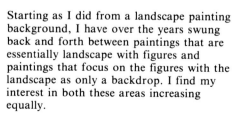

9

Starting as I did from a landscape painting background, I have over the years swung back and forth between paintings that are essentially landscape with figures and paintings that focus on the figures with the landscape as only a backdrop. I find my interest in both these areas increasing equally.

12

14

15

17

16

18

19

10

An old Mennonite woman who saw this painting of the Meetinghouse said to me that it represented to her all of life and death. She added, "Even the backhouse shows the common round, the daily task". People often open my eyes to my own paintings. Painted in oil in 1967, it has the strong style that was encouraged at art college.

23

24

21

22

25

26

27

Over the years as I have driven around Mennonite country I have become aware of the many dog families. While the Amish farmers favour smallish light-coloured dogs, the Mennonites own larger collie-St. Bernard-crossed dogs. In all cases these dogs are the Heinz 57 variety. No pure-bred inbreds for them. Hybrid vigour is the order of the day.

29

30

28

31

32

33

34

35

36

My Grandfather Snyder was known as
"Apple Noah". Besides the mixed farming
typical of most Mennonites, he also tended a
large apple orchard. How strong in my
memory is the smell of apples in the garage
and the aroma of apple schnitz in the attic as
Grandma hung them in cloth bags. Even as I
write these lines, I munch on an apple,
thinking of the past.

38

39

40

41

Remember lunch in a honey pail and sandwiches wrapped in waxed paper? These Mennonite kids carry store-bought lunch pails, another sign of the relaxation of severe standards. The games they play as they walk the roads and the fields to and from school, however, are the same as those played many years ago.

43

The Milverton Mill brings to mind the first time that, as a young Toronto art student, I went to the meeting room of the Elmira Mill. It was here, next to the horse shed, that farmers and retired farmers gathered to set the world right. Because the conversation moved quickly in Pennsylvania Dutch, I was doomed to strain to catch the meaning, to stay with the conversation. My situation was made worse because I did not know the verbal shorthand that existed in this group, as in any, in a small town.

42

44

45

46

A pony cart is a much more common sight today than it was twenty years ago.

As some of the Mennonite groups become less conservative, more frivolous activities become acceptable. Also, I suppose the start of the parochial schools ten years ago is a factor in the spread of the popularity of these small carts. Sometimes in winter the pony becomes the engine to pull a skier. Even in a closed society things change — slowly, but they change.

47

48

49

50

51

52

54

53

55

The Team at Bat is an idea that I have worked on for five or six years. For several years I have had this preliminary painting nailed up on my studio wall. From time to time I add or subtract. Someday I hope that it will become part of a set; the Team at Bat, the Team in the Field. Who knows?

56

57

58

59

60

61

I gave this painting to my wife for her 35th birthday. Unfortunately over the years I have not kept many of my paintings. In the early years we needed the money so badly that I had to sell a painting when I had a chance. I only managed to stay in the art business because my wife had a job as a children's library assistant.

63

64

65

I often use small animals or birds as a design element in a painting. Sometimes a tiny form will enhance a composition. Although from a handling standpoint chickens are not fun, their colouring and shape can be most attractive.

68

67

69

Aside from a few early French Canadian paintings of skating, Currier and Ives seem to be about the only North American artists who have done much with that topic. I find it strange that in a northern region where almost everyone has skated, there are so few paintings of the sport.

71

70

74

75

76

77

78

79

80

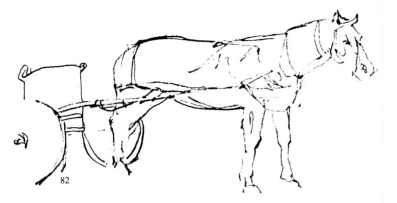
82

83

84

85

Riding in a buggy, even with a frisky horse,
is a leisurely experience. It provides an
opportunity to look, to evaluate, and to
think. I suppose to compare the
contemplative time of the Mennonites to the
Far Eastern religions is an overstatement, but
that slower-paced nineteenth-century lifestyle
does allow for much time for thought. I am
sometimes most surprised by the questions
asked or the conjectures posed by a
Mennonite farmer. From foreign policy to
race relations to philosophy, these questions
are carefully considered and digested.

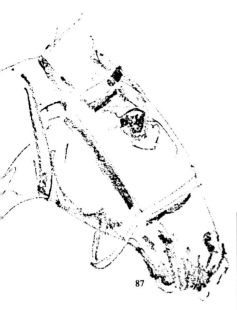

87

88

89

Of all the specialized pictures of the Mennonites, few can compare with the horses at the Meetinghouse. This every-second-Sunday occurrence draws people's attention and interest. This subject, so romantic from the outside, is most serious from the inside. Services in Pennsylvania Dutch that last for two hours are the norm. The congregation is admonished by several preachers and are led in long prayers while kneeling on the wooden church floor.

Although the Older-Order Mennonites met in little clapboard churches, the Older-Order Amish meet in the homes of members. This ultra-conservative order must, of course, have small groups. In most other areas of life the conservative Mennonite and Amish groups are similar, varying only on small points of dress and custom.

90

91

92

93

94

96

95

Although I've always felt drawing to be a most expressive component of my painting, I have not pursued drawing on its own as much as I should have done. Ten years ago I stumbled onto the scratcher board idea. Quite common in the nineteenth century, this process is now seldom used. By drawing on a board that has been paved with a chalky substance, the drawing is started. The next step, a reductive one, allows the artist to scratch out or cross-hatch some previously inked areas. It makes me more relaxed to know that I can correct an area or develop a reverse pattern in white over the black lines I have penned.

97

98

99

Character studies such as these are enjoyable capsules that I store for use in future paintings. Because my paintings are always a group of ideas and images, I hoard motifs and vignettes for the right moment. So often several ideas can be organized and presented in such a way that the sum is more than its parts. I am developing a design now of an almost all-Mennonite auction sale in which I think can make good use of these two studies.

100

101

102

103

104

105

106

107

108

109

In any painting I seek a hook or an angle much like a writer does. That point of view or unexpected twist can cause the viewer to consider the subject in a new light. If the approach is really good, the viewer will not be conscious of the manipulation. Weather conditions, juxtapositioning of characters, elevating or lowering visual point of view as well as the focusing in or out of the subjects are among the devices that I use.

110

Although maple syrup is a traditional cash crop, the customary tree-hung pails are, in most areas of eastern Canada, giving way to pipelines that sway through the bush. The elimination of the labour-intensive, burdensome aspects of this chore makes financial sense. I am pleased to report that in the more conservative Mennonite groups where manpower is not so short and where rigorous physical work is regarded almost as a challenge, the traditional approach survives.

111

112

48

114

115

116

117

119

118

52

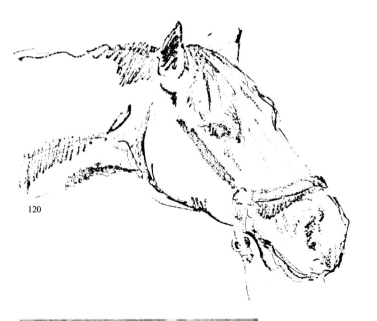

120

To my eye, the more interesting images that occur are those small pieces of business that happen on the sidelines, secondary to the main action. I look for those secondary poses, those insights into human nature, the same way a playwright or actor must. So often a pose will reveal more than all the action in the world.

A natural pose poorly painted is far more revealing than a posed stance expertly executed.

121

122

123

124

The Mennonites of Waterloo County are so like the rural Europeans, especially those of Germany: the short, broad physique, the industrious attitude, the choice of food, and even some clothing. The edge of the cap bound with grosgrain ribbon is typical of Bavaria but is found for sale at the Linwood General Store only ten minutes from my studio.

126

125

129

Although I now work from scenes or situations that I observe, years ago I sometimes started out with an idea and then searched for the site to fit that concept. I'm sure I passed up many potential paintings because I was out looking for a location or activity to suit my preconceived idea. Now I often simply drive or walk about the country waiting for a scene to present itself or any activity to happen. Almost all my inspiration is just a happy accident. I must learn to be more aware of what I see. Only in commissioned paintings do I go looking for set pieces, but even then the painting is made viable by a chance bit of business at the site.

128

130

131

Whenever I exhibit my paintings, a small group of bridge connoisseurs shows up. Although there are few cement bridges left in Ontario, I am amazed at the number of people whose relatives were involved in cement bridge building. To me a bridge is simply the junction box of stream and road and as such provides many possible subjects to paint.

This small cement bridge is just north of Waterloo and leads to one of the prettiest farms in Waterloo County.

132

133

134

135

137

The success of this reproduction was a pleasant surprise to me. Although I find many aspects of traditional farm life interesting, I was not sure that an image of preparing the Thanksgiving fowl would find such acceptance. Some accounts of common everyday farm activities strike urban people as either cruel and distasteful or charming and romantic. Because I have a foot in both rural and urban camps, I often see both sides.

136

138

139

140

141

142

143

Life on a mixed farm offers me so many topics that are well worth painting. Although not the magnificent beasts of Landseer, domestic farm animals are a good source of subjects. Often I use the animals as secondary themes in paintings, but much time could be profitably spent featuring these creatures. I do not mean the cloying Victorian treatment of animals but rather the description of the animals' instinctive behavior.

144

146

Shown below is a double tandem hitch. This drawing is an attempt to demonstrate the vigour of the various elements in this motif. I have many books filled with sketches or gesture drawings that are finished works and also may be used as notes to myself. Although I use photographs to give me detailed information, I need to translate these facts into an energetic design. I am not painting the objects, I am making a picture.

147

148

149

150

151

This quick pencil drawing gropes for the motion and attitude of the man. I try to discover in a gesture an insight into the person. I think this drawing quite revealing.

153

Pictured here is one of the back-breaking jobs on the farm. The use of lower wagons for corn harvest does ease the strain, but after thirty acres of stooping, the end of the field is welcome. The location of this loosely painted rendition is near Crosshill, Ontario.

152

154

155

156

Tucked deep in the hills between Linwood and Crosshill lie several concessions that are home to some very conservative Mennonite families. Along those roads there are neither hydro nor telephone wires. To wait for only a few minutes is to witness rural life as it was lived a century ago. Oh true, there are some small changes in the farm equipment, some jerry-built implements caused by the non-existence of new parts for these ancient machines. But the main fabric of the agricultural family, with its dependence on neighbourly co-operation, is still intact.

157

159

161

162

160

163

I've always admired Albert Franks's paintings of the old Toronto row houses. It seems to me that the Mennonite farmhouse with its various additions has a similar possibility. In the coming years I am going to pursue this idea in both paintings and drawings. The longer I live, the longer becomes the list of good topics that I wish to pursue. How very lucky I am that I have possibilities that pull me along. The trick is to control the team and not find yourself gripping the reins of runaways.

164

165

166

167

If somehow the gods conspire against you, then sometimes they also come to your aid. In 1980 when I painted the *Country Mailboxes* all the pieces fell so smoothly into place. Seldom have I painted over my head to such a degree. Perhaps only in *Gathering at the Meetinghouse* was I fortunate enough to experience an equally almost mystical experience. It is no accident that I still own both these paintings.

169

170

168

172

One of the most pleasant memories from my childhood was the arrival every week of *The Saturday Evening Post*. The Norman Rockwell covers and the story illustrations inside influenced me very strongly. In my early teen years I discovered the American illustrators of the twenties and thirties — Pyle, Wyeth, the Leyendecker brothers. At art college I became familiar with the work of the French Impressionists, the Luminists, the Hudson River School and the American Impressionists.

Now as I travel, I seek out paintings that were once denigrated by the term "illustration". I love the stuff and it shows in my own work. I am happy for that evidence.

173

174

175

79

176

I am astonished at how the horse sale at Carson's, near Listowel, parallels the country horse fairs painted by Sir Alfred Munnings, P.R.A., before the turn of the century. True, the people are dressed differently. But the excitement generated by snapping tent canvas, the whinnying of the horses, the shouting of the people and the changing of the sunlight is strongly reminiscent of those magnificent paintings.

177

178

179

180

Although I have worked on this painting on and off for five years, it is still not finished. I tried to infuse this painting with the excitement of a three-ring circus. The practice ring of the Royal Winter Fair is one of my favourites. With competitors for various classes either warming up or lining up, it is a jumble of images. In the future I intend to do more things of competitive horse events. Also on my list of topics is the shed row area of horse race tracks. Years ago Sir Alfred Munnings painted the English racing scene so well that it fires me up to give that idea a try.

181

184

183

185

The world of horse shows is attractive to me. Perhaps because our family used to show draft horses at small shows and fairs, I am drawn to these activities. In those days the local companies, such as our dairy, used horse shows and parades as advertising opportunities. Now, as I prowl the Royal, those smells, sounds, and activities trigger a nostalgia in me. Although I want to draw and paint these scenes, I find it difficult to apply myself to the painting. So easily I drift away from the easel and become part of the scene that I should be recording.

186

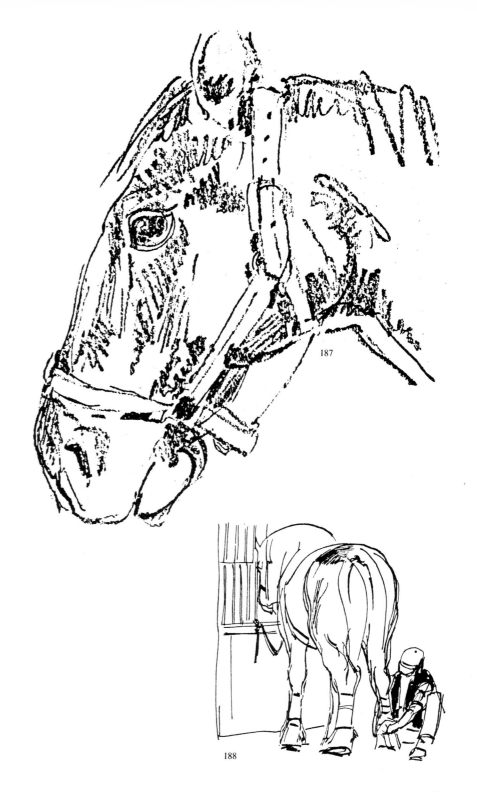

187

188

For some reason I have always been drawn to architecture as a subject. As an art student in Toronto I hung around with an architecture student. A glimpse into the course of study required by his program convinced me that I had not the discipline necessary to master the math and physics. I now build new buildings and old in paint with no concern for stress, span, or budget.

189

190

191

I can remember that as a child I trailed along with my Grandfather as he scythed the verge beside the laneway. So often I find echoes of my childhood in the topics that I select to paint. Although the actual men I picture here are from Upper Canada Village in Morrisburg, Ontario, I'm sure one is also my Grandfather.

193

194

195

My willingness to enter into the game of the pioneer villages makes it possible for me to step back in time. Across North America and Europe there are so many marvellous historic re-creations. How lucky for me that so much effort and money have been spent to re-create this world. Possible paintings crowd my mind after a day at an historic spot.

196

197

198

199

201

Among those ideas that I pursue in paint is
the antique still life. For me it combines the
joys of composition as I arrange and
rearrange the pieces and the pleasure of the
actual pieces themselves. The sleighbells
I bought from an Old-Order Mennonite farmer
23 years ago, the lantern at an auction 20
years ago. The small kettle came from an
antique store 15 years ago, and, soon after,
I bought the brass grain scoop in England.
How often those pieces could be regrouped
and lighted differently to create entirely new
visual displays.

202

203

In Virginia I feel the union of North America
and England. A place like historic
Williamsburg makes that combination
obvious. Since things English and historic
appeal to me, it is not terribly surprising that
I continue to return to this historic spot.
I would like to do more paintings of this
small slice of North America's past.

204

205

206

207

At historic Williamsburg, Va., the landscape joins forces with the architecture to form such a suitable setting for the costumes and the crafts. When we return north I am always struck by the harshness of our area in contrast to the softness and elegance of the historic South.

208

209

210

211

Growing up as I did in a Mennonite home, I had no concept of rest and relaxation. How fortunate Marilyn and I were to get to know people who own a weekend country house. Although not grand, their stone building is crammed with interesting antiques, each with its own story. One of the weekend's regular activities is designing and rearranging the garden. Our English travels reinforce this experience. We have started our own English Country Garden. Thank you, David, Sally, and Nora.

213

212

214

216

For several years I kept, in my file, some photos of workmen eating lunch outside. From time to time I was tempted to use this motif with a different setting but held back, waiting for the right time. I'm glad that I waited to use this scene outside the Seagram Distillery (circa 1881). It was past this very spot that my brothers and I walked on our way to church or to my Grandmother's house after she moved to town from the farm.

215

218

For many years I have kept coming back to this tiny mill. When I was a teenager, this building provided a subject both romantic and simple. As I worked my way through Art College, the uniqueness of the spot appealed to me. Over the last twenty years I have drawn and painted this mill over twenty times. Sometimes the focus of my painting is the mill, sometimes the landscape. The marshy area around abounds in wildlife. Each passing season and light effect provide new shades to this country cathedral near Blair, Ontario.

219

220

In my time with Grand Valley Conservation Foundation I've been led to many small country stores. Although not quite the general stores of the Mennonite Country type, these tiny stores hold a vast collection of items. In these stores, too, as in the Mennonite farmhouses, we see the vernacular achitecture. Made up of additions and sheds and porches, this building has been adapted to many generations and many uses.

222

223

105

224

How often I find the scene of the backs of buildings more interesting than the main street view. Because the sight of the rear is less predictable, I find that I see it better. For the artist, the difference between looking and seeing is immense. Along the river course, I see with a new eye and find those landscapes engaging. Because it takes energy to really observe, I must constantly guard against lazy vision. Ironically, when I discover a site that energizes me, the adrenalin flows and I go on to explore more prospects until I almost literally drop.

225

226

228

229

227

230

231

232

233

234

235

My interest in landscapes and old mills often takes me into fisherman's territory. I am amazed at how careful and contemplative the fisherman is. Many of these fellows (I see few women) seem perfectly content to stand or sit by a brook for hours, smoking their pipes.
I pause and then pass, seldom talking.
To these men, fishing is bliss; to me, fishing is just drowning worms.

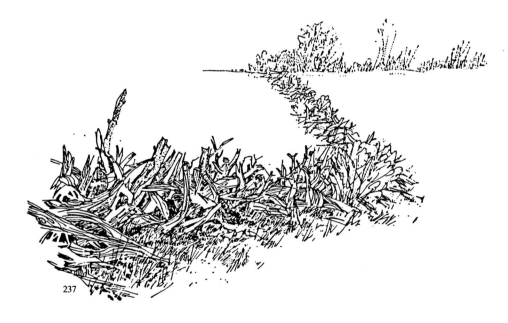

237

236

239

240

241

Rail fences, once so common, are now seldom seen even in Mennonite country. Because a snake-style fence with its accompanying fence row takes so much land, modern efficient farmers have swept them away. However, in areas where the land is graded number two, one can still see the "silver snakes".

243

242

244

245

Most of my painting deals with light and its effect on objects. The inclusion of water and its sparkling quality allows me to bounce light back and forth across a painting. I hope to draw the viewer into the effect without his being conscious of my manipulation.

247

248

Patterns set up by weeds and rushes often
develop into a very strong counterpoint to
the main theme of a painting. Because I
work intuitively, adding and subtracting as
I go along, a clump of grasses that starts out
as a very secondary area in a painting can
become much more dominant than I had
originally intended.

250

"If the dog could talk what a tale he'd tell" is a line from a song, but applies as well to the massive stone mills. Among the earliest businesses started in any settled area, the mill provided a meeting place as well as a product. As the Grand River winds south on its way to Lake Erie, it flows through towns like Fergus and past mills like the one pictured below.

252

253

The covered bridge at West Montrose, the last covered bridge in Ontario, is without doubt the building that most people wish to see in my paintings. This romantic structure draws people from all over the continent. Because the bridge is such a long wiener, it makes composition very difficult. Due to the restricted access on the banks, a view of the bridge from nearby is tough. Down the river

255

256

from the west side there is a large hill which provides a marvellous view of bridge and valley. As often happens, the presence of the bridge makes people blind to the pretty little village itself.

257

Although I sometimes paint from my mobile studio, I often paint outside. My window van with the easel inside protects me from the weather, wind and gawkers. I've never had enough courage to implement a device about which I read. An artist placed his cap next to the easel as he sketched outside and in his cap he put some money. When a chatty hiker would come by, the man would simply smile and point towards his hat.

258

262

263

Not until I got into my third year at Ontario College of Art did the penny drop for me about drawing. I was a slow starter on that front and I still find that I must keep working on it. When I see some of the beautiful drawings by early magazine illustrators, it becomes apparent to me how far I have to go. The days before colour reproductions were everywhere, the ability to control a pen drawing was a huge asset for an artist. I was pleased to have had the chance in the last year to show my *Valley Sketchbook* series in nineteen newspapers along the Grand River. In an odd sort of way it put me back to those days when drawing was king.

266

267

265

The area along a small creek provides many features to paint. I stalk small waterways looking for fallen logs, interesting groups of weeds and grasses, unusual rocks, small rapids or falls, appealing banks, and washouts. All these features, when strafed by light, are attractive. Often a setting for a major painting comes out of an afternoon spent prowling a stream.

270

269

273

274

275

138

276

277

278

280

Near Fairy Cottage in the Sussex coastal town of Rye this boat sits beached, waiting for new paint. In 1979 Marilyn and I spent several weeks in a 16th-century house in this small town. From Oak Corner I could walk or drive out with my painting gear to capture images that stood still, waiting to be caught.

282

281

141

This windmill is not in Holland. Located near the town of Rye, Sussex, U.K., this mill was built several hundred years ago to pump water from the Romney marsh. Today that marsh is a large basin of fruitful farmland.

284

283

285

286

Painted on a beautiful summer morning at Nare Head on the south coast of England, this painting is totally different from the one I painted the previous day during a storm on this beach. That same trip we visited the towering cliffs at Tintagel, which tradition says was the home of King Arthur.

287

143

288

I suppose it is the romance of history that I find so appealing. When we travel, my drawings or paintings almost always focus on the historic and, many times, on the downright broken down. Perhaps it's an insecurity within me that draws me to the continuity and certainty of a tried and proven look in design...I don't know.

289

290

291

292

When we returned from our first trip to Europe in 1966, I painted a group of paintings that recorded some of the places and views that we had seen. This view from our window in Barcelona is a massive painting which I am pleased I still own. The 1967 show of these paintings in Kitchener was a total failure. At that point I was distraught that no one wanted my bits of Europe; now I am pleased that they didn't.

293

294

295

This acrylic sketch shows a small backwater
town near historic Williamsburg, Va.
It stands very nicely in counterpoint to a bit
of Bermuda (on the right) and a rear view of
old buildings in New Hamburg, Ontario.
Part of an artist's style is his subject
selection. It seems to me that my approach
to diverse geography shows itself on these
pages.

296

297

Set high on a mountain overlooking Merano, Castle Freiburg hosts travellers from around the world. It was once the summer home and fortress of an Italian family; now it is a hotel. Among the prettiest hotels that I have stayed in, this building looks down on a panorama of towns, villages, and vineyards.

298

299

301

302

303

304

Set on a hill, the town of Rye, Sussex, was used for centuries as a military installation and defensive post. At the centre of this town is the church square. Since the town is so ancient, those houses surrounding the church yard are historic and picturesque.

305

306

308

309

310

311

312

314

313

The flowers and the architecture of villages both here and abroad put me in mind of pictures from children's books. Very often the residents of a village are embarrassed about some feature that seems to me most charming. In these small villages there is a sense for me of things being not quite real.

315

316

317

318

319

I set up my easel in a corner of the white
garden at Sissinghurst Castle in England.
As I stood quietly painting on this June
afternoon, not one Englishman spoke to me.
In North America an artist will draw a group
and many questions. In England people may
pause slightly but will continue on their way
without a word. On a table next to us at
dinner that night there was a sign that I
thought summed up the British — Reserved.

320

Biography

I do not mourn the slowing of grants to painters; in fact I would argue that much government support actually weakens the artist's contact with the public. Government assumes a superior attitude to the public. Somehow the great unwashed are not competent to decide if they can respond responsibly to an artist's work. They feel that we need a bureaucrat to decide whose work should be supported. In those early years of my career I would have been most happy to receive a grant, but I realize now that in the long run my efforts for response to my work would have been directed to those grant givers and not to my true audience, the public. Unfortunately we have built up a system that sees as synonymous grants and awards. Many artists put forward as their main credential the number of grants that they have received. They view grants as prizes bestowed by some all-knowing cultural officer. It seems to me only when an artist can stir people's hearts and minds can he be deemed a success. I want to touch more people than a few professional art pundits. Perhaps because of my Mennonite background, where rank is discouraged, or perhaps because I am unsophisticated, I choose to take my chances with the public. I think the example of a self-sustaining artist that I found as a

teenager when I took painting lessons from Matthew Kousal started me believing that independence was possible. Through the latter years of high school and three years at Ontario College of Art I managed to sell my paintings. The prices were reasonable and I developed a respect for people's response to my work. It was, therefore, disheartening when the exhibition of paintings that I held following our first trip to Europe was totally rejected by the public. I sold nothing at all and was given no hope to believe that what had so enthused me about Europe held any appeal for anyone else. I realize now that those paintings were rather poor executions of subjects with which I was not at all familiar.

Following that disaster, I joined forces with another former student of Mr. Kousal's, Mike Roth. Together we shared a studio above a shoe store in Waterloo, and from there we sallied forth to stage shows of our paintings in shopping malls in both Ontario and the northern United States. We were quite successful with our landscape paintings of Northern Ontario. However, life on the road selling paintings that did not sufficiently move me was not satisfying. A few years earlier I had painted images of the Mennonites of northern Waterloo County. I longed to return to that subject. My wife's encouragement was all that I needed to start on a track that led me to my present situation.

We bought an old house with tenants on the top floor and Marilyn and I lived on the main floor. I had my studio/gallery/classroom in the basement. Through the recommendation of one of my students, the director of Eaton's College Street Gallery arrived at my basement door. He liked what he saw and within a week I found my paintings hung at that gallery in Toronto. My things were hung in a small side room, not in the main display space. Even so, I thought that I had died and gone to heaven. The exposure at an old established gallery like that was enormous. With time, sufficient interest by the public in my work helped ease my paintings into the main galleries and then into a one-man show. Although things were going very well I noticed that, as the managers changed quickly over the next two years, the standards and tone of the gallery diminished. It became apparent to me that as an artist I was only as secure as the gallery in which I showed. When the umpteenth new manager arrived on the scene and announced that because it was spring he would only exhibit paintings of spring, I knew that it was time to leave.

I tried other galleries but found between high commissions (40% of retail), crooked gallery owners, and petty gallery politics, this scene was not for me. In 1972 Marilyn and I asked our tenants to leave and took over the entire house, using the additional space as a gallery. The small gallery that we had then, open only by appointment, gave way three years later to a gallery open regular business hours. We started to sell reproductions of black and white drawings and a few coloured limited edition reproductions. We hired help to staff the gallery so that we were free to pursue the muse. That was a fortunate decision. How easy it would have been to have found myself trapped in a shop rather than being free to prowl Mennonite country. Following a one-day-a-week stint as artist-in-residence at Conrad Grebel College, University of Waterloo, I teamed up with an old classmate from high school days to produce a book, *Mennonite Country, Waterloo County Drawings by Peter Etril Snyder*. During these first ten years of our marriage we travelled to Europe and England as money allowed. For us, this was a priority. A one-man show at Ontario House, London, England, was held in 1979. All along the way I was building an audience and I listened to their response. By this point we had expanded the group of limited edition reproductions that we sold at our shop and to a few wholesale accounts, with my brother Doug working part-time. When Doug came with us full time I was finally able to get away almost entirely from the day-to-day grind of the shop. Shortly after that time Christian Bell Porcelain approached me for a set of twelve designs to be used for collectors' plates. The exposure brought to my work by the reproductions, our annual catalogue, and the collectors' plates dramatically increased the number of people who knew my work. I hope that people who see this book will respond because public response affects me so much as an artist.

Index of Figures

All works are acrylic unless otherwise stated.

No.	Title	Year	Size
232	Mennonite Farm near St. Jacobs	1975	8″ × 10″
233	Downstream, *detail*	1984	36″ × 48″
234	Quiet Creek	1982	12″ × 16″
235	Fishing at Hortop Mill, *detail* (ink on scratcher board)	1985	10″ × 12″
236	Near the Farmers' Market	1985	20″ × 16″
237	Stump Fence (ink of scratcher board)	1985	8″ × 10″
238	House, Girls from the Pony Cart	1982	18″ × 24″
239	Fishing at Everton, Ontario	1985	24″ × 18″
240	Hortop Mill	1985	8″ × 10″
241	Beaver Dam in the Gatineaux	1986	12″ × 16″
242	King's Landing, *detail*	1985	18″ × 24″
243	Four Horse Hitch, *detail*	1984	24″ × 36″
244	Branches (pencil)	1980	6″ × 8″
245	Drifting Snow	1985	12″ × 16″
246	Credit River at Cataract, *detail*	1984	30″ × 40″
247	Patterns of Light & Dark	1982	12″ × 16″
248	Credit River at Cataract, *detail*	1984	30″ × 40″
249	Falls on the Oxtongue, *detail*	1985	18″ × 24″
250	Favourite Fishing Spot, *detail*	1985	12″ × 16″
251	Mill on the Raisin River, *detail*	1985	18″ × 24″
252	Fergus Mill (watercolour & carbon pencil)	1984	10″ × 12″
253	Fergus Mill	1982	12″ × 16″
254	Conestogo River, East of Hawkesville	1984	12″ × 16″
255	Covered Bridge (ink on scratcher board)	1985	10″ × 12″
256	Grazing on the Flat	1982	12″ × 16″
257	Drawing on Trees (pen & ink)	1977	8″ × 10″
258	Near Hope, B.C.	1986	6″ × 8″
259	Cottage Road, *detail*	1985	24″ × 32″
260	Late Spring at Elora Gorge, *detail*	1984	24″ × 32″
261	Design for Glacial Lake #284 (pen & ink)	1983	8″ × 10″
262	Late Spring at Elora Gorge, *detail*	1984	24″ × 32″
263	Fergus Mill (ink on scratcher board)	1985	10″ × 12″
264	Late Spring at Elora Gorge, *detail*	1984	24″ × 32″
265	Near Erbsville (pencil)	1984	8″ × 10″
266	Study of Williamsburg, Va.	1980	8″ × 10″
267	Near Williamsburg, Va.	1980	8″ × 10″
268	Young Street, Waterloo (pen & ink)	1984	8″ × 10″
269	Winter Stream (ink on scratcher board)	1985	8″ × 10″
270	Winter Stream	1982	12″ × 16″
271	Silvery Light, Hopewell Creek	1984	16″ × 20″
272	Highway #7, B.C.	1986	24″ × 36″
273	Field Sketch near Banff	1980	8″ × 10″
274	Field Sketch near Banff	1980	8″ × 10″
275	Vancouver (pen & ink)	1983	8″ × 10″
276	Glacial Lake	1985	12″ × 16″
277	Field Sketch near Banff	1980	8″ × 10″
278	Marina, Vancouver	1983	8″ × 10″
279	Boat Repairs, Peggy's Cove, *detail*	1984	18″ × 24″
280	Dry Dock, Rye, Sussex	1979	8″ × 10″
281	Dry Dock, Port Maitland (ink on scratcher board)	1985	10″ × 12″
282	Boat Repairs, Peggy's Cove, *detail*	1984	18″ × 24″
283	The Priory Hotel, Bath, England	1978	8″ × 10″
284	Windmill at Rye	1979	8″ × 10″
285	Border Country, U.K. (pen & ink)	1983	8″ × 10″
286	Doorway at Perouges, France (pen & ink)	1976	4″ × 5″
287	Nare Head, England	1972	9″ × 12″
288	Churchyard at Rye, Sussex	1979	8″ × 10″
289	Florence, Italy (watercolour)	1982	8″ × 10″
290	Lower Slaughter, Cotswolds England (pencil)	1978	8″ × 10″
291	Church, France (pen & ink)	1976	8″ × 10″
292	Mill Ruins at Doon	1970	16″ × 20″
293	Barcelona	1967	40″ × 40″
294	New Hamburg, Ontario (pen & ink)	1982	8″ × 10″
295	Study of Village in Virginia	1980	8″ × 10″
296	Bermuda's Doorway	1980	8″ × 10″
297	Village Church, England (watercolour)	1971	9″ × 12″
298	Church Carving (pen & ink)	1984	4″ × 6″
299	Italy	1982	8″ × 10″
300	Backyards, Amsterdam	1967	20″ × 24″
301	Rye, Sussex	1979	8″ × 10″
302	Just off Great Russell Sq., London, England	1967	8″ × 10″
303	Italy (pen & ink)	1982	8″ × 10″
304	Church Square, Rye, Sussex	1979	8″ × 10″
305	Hotel Courtyard, Paris (pen & ink)	1977	8″ × 10″
306	Timber Houses, Rye, Sussex	1979	10″ × 20″
307	Small Harbour, Bermuda	1980	8″ × 10″
308	Small Harbour (scratcher board)	1985	8″ × 10″
309	Bermuda View	1980	8″ × 10″
310	Perouges Street, France	1976	8″ × 10″
311	Green Umbrellas, Portugal	1967	8″ × 16″
312	Paris, France	1976	8″ × 10″
313	Daisy & Petunia	1985	16″ × 12″
314	Troutbeck, Lake District, England (watercolour)	1977	9″ × 12″
315	Piddlehinton, England (pencil)	1972	10″ × 12″
316	View from the Wall, Rye, England	1979	8″ × 10″
317	Drawing of Flowers (pen & ink)	1985	6″ × 8″
318	Edge of Garden	1985	6″ × 8″
319	White Garden, Sissinghurst Castle, England	1976	8″ × 10″
320	Tiger Lillies	1984	8″ × 10″

Peter Etril Snyder's works—paintings, drawings, and prints—
are available at his studio, 59 Erb Street East, Waterloo, Ontario.

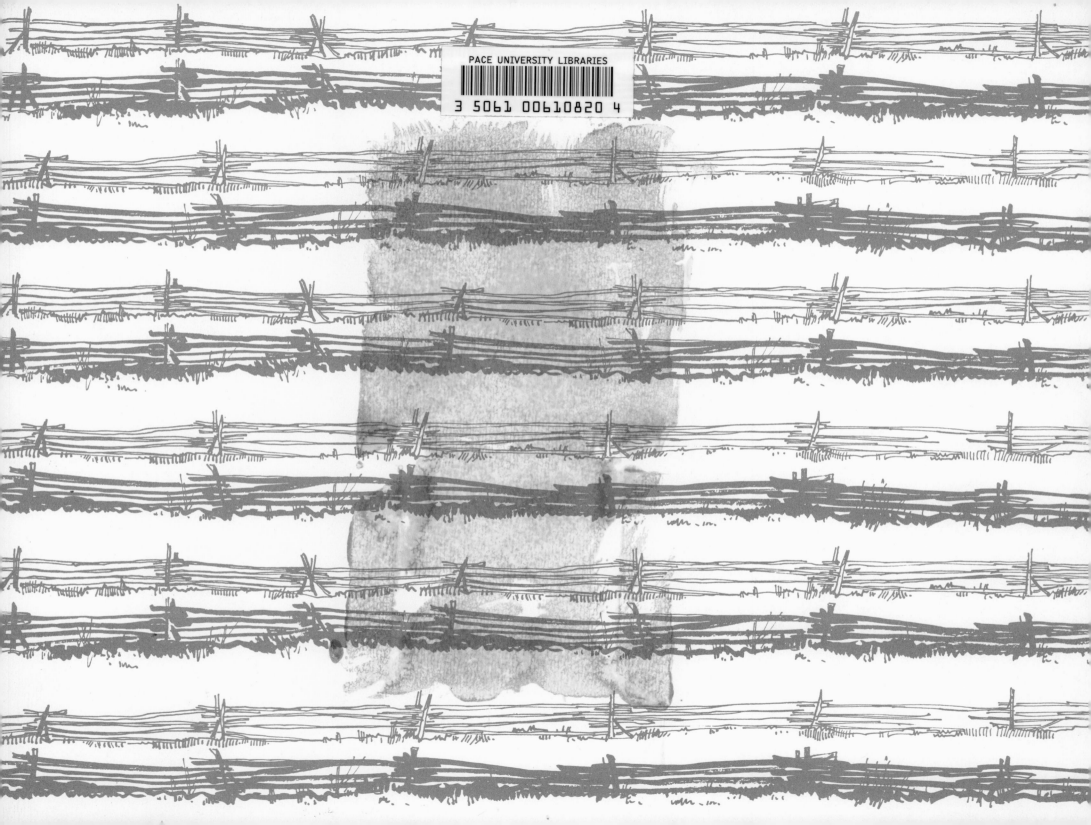